Jesse Lemuel Delano

A Record of Sunderland in the Civil War of 1861-1865

Jesse Lemuel Delano

A Record of Sunderland in the Civil War of 1861-1865

ISBN/EAN: 9783337222321

Printed in Europe, USA, Canada, Australia, Japan

Cover: Foto ©ninafisch / pixelio.de

More available books at **www.hansebooks.com**

A RECORD

OF

SUNDERLAND IN THE CIVIL WAR

OF 1861 TO 1865.

COMPILED BY

— JESSE L. DELANO, —

IN 1881.

ACCORDING TO VOTE OF THE TOWN.

AMHERST, MASS.
J. E. WILLIAMS, PRINTER.
1882.

OF

SUNDERLAND IN THE CIVIL WAR

OF 1861 TO 1865.

COMPILED BY

— JESSE L. DELANO,

IN 1881.

ACCORDING TO VOTE OF THE TOWN.

AMHERST, MASS.
J. E. WILLIAMS, PRINTER.
1882.

INTRODUCTION.

In 1863 the Legislature of Massachusetts voted that each
town should make a record of its soldiers, and of such facts
relating to each and his service as might be interesting or
useful to future generations. For various reasons our town
neglected to make such a record at that time, and there-
fore, after long delay, in 1880 the town voted that such a
record be made, so far as possible, and placed among the
other records of the town for preservation. After considerable investigation and research, the vote has been com-
plied with, and according to a vote of the town in March,
1882, abstracts of the same—together with some explanatory
and historical narrative—is now presented to the public.

RECORD.

On the 12th of April 1861, the cannon of nineteen batteries rained a torrent of shot and shell on the devoted heads of sixty beseiged and half-starved men in Fort Sumter, S. C., who stood true to their Country and had not forsaken their post even when their last biscuit was eaten. Those rebel guns battered down and set on fire the fort, compelled the surrender of the heroes, and while in the Providence of God they took not the life of a single man, they nevertheless accomplished their mission. The people heard them breaking down the great Temple of Liberty and Union which their Fathers had builded, and they roused themselves like a giant from his sleep, and the shots that were intended to sever this nation in twain, only tended to cement firmly together all loyal hearts and hands throughout the land. The men buckled on the armor of the patriot, and grasped the sword and musket, while the women in tears, bade them go forth to fight, stayed behind to watch, and work, and pray, and wait, for nearly five long years.

There are some among us who remember well the exciting events of those days and months after the fall of Fort Sumter, when the work of preparation—both of men and material—was being pushed to the utmost: when meetings were held all over the country—when volunteers offered themselves by the thousand—when men were drafted, and bought and hired, when money was poured out by the

million—when blood flowed like water—when anxious faces
dreaded to hear the next day's news, and when, alas, too
often, the worst fears of the weeping ones were realized.

Aye, *there are a few* among us now who can sit calmly
down, and *recall*, as it were a dream, the glittering parade,
the mustering camp, the crowded transport, the watchful
picket line, the dusty and wearisome march, the assault so
deadly, the smoke and din of battle, the hospital, the surgeon's knife, the letters from home, the prison pen, the dead
comrade's face, and the final victory.

Yes, there are some here *now*, who remember all this and
more, but the number is growing smaller year by year, and
in a few years more none will be left to tell the tale.

In the years to come, when the favored sons and daugh-
ters of Sunderland are asked the questions " What part did
your town bear in the suppression of the Great Rebellion,
and did anybody go out from you to stay the mad hand of
Treason?" " Did your town furnish any aid to those who
entered the army? Did *any* lay down their lives for their
Country?" it should be the pride and glory of all to be able
to answer in the affirmative, and point to the Record of
noble action, both of those who went to the front, and those
who followed them with their gifts and prayers. That we
may be able to answer such questions intelligently, and to
preserve from oblivion the names of those who took their
lives in their hands and went forth at the call of duty, and
the liberal means furnished by the town for their comfort,
and for aid to their families in their absence, is the object
of the investigation which has been made, and the result of
which is embodied in the Record which is now presented to
you. It is a matter of regret that this Record was not
attended to before. Twenty years work wondrous changes,
and many things, *once* easily ascertained, are *now* obtained
with difficulty, and in some cases with considerable expense,

while other matters also quite desirable cannot be found. Realizing these difficulties it was with much hesitation that the work was commenced, and though not as complete and full as desirable, still we have a Record, that for all practical purposes will probably be sufficient.

The people of Sunderland were united in their efforts to do their part in providing men and means, and numerous meetings, both of the town and of the people, were held to accomplish the purpose, and the war and its progress was the all-absorbing topic in private and in public.

The valuation of the town of Sunderland in 1860 was $345,843; in 1865 it was $412,827. The whole amount of money expended as a town on account of the war, exclusive of State aid to soldiers' families, was $12,490.52, which is nearly four per cent. of the town valuation. The sums also raised and expended by the town, for aid to the families of soldiers during the years of the war, were as follows: In 1861. $23.92; in 1862, $624.40; in 1863, $1486.80; in 1864, $840.44; in 1865, $543.56, making a total of State Aid during the five years of $3,519.12. This was afterwards repaid by the Commonwealth. In 1880 state aid had dwindled to $192, and only two recipients. The labor of arranging the details of all these extra expenses, and of securing the men who should enlist to the credit of the town, and of disbursing the funds to their families, fell in a great measure on the officers of the town, who were unremittent in their work, and expended much time and labor without compensation. The selectmen in 1861 were D. Dwight Whitmore, John R. Smith, and Albert Montague; in 1862. Albert Montague, Elihu Smith, and George L. Bachelder; in 1864, Albert Montague, Erastus Pomeroy, Stoughton D. Crocker; in 1865, Albert Montague, Henry J. Graves and Merrick Montague. The Town Clerk during all these years was Horace W. Taft. The Town

Treasurer of 1861 was William Hunt; in 1863. 1864 and 1865 John M. Smith.

The first town meeting at which any action was taken in reference to the subject was held the 24th of May. 1861. and it was voted: "That Charles Whitmore. James B. Prouty. Samuel Jennison. N. Austin Smith. Israel Childs and Charles Cooley be a committee to disburse such sums as shall, in their judgment. be necessary for an outfit for any persons. residents of this town. who may enlist for the support and defense of our Union and for the comfort of their families during their term of service. and that said Committee be authorized to borrow such sum or sums, not exceeding two thousand dollars. as shall be necessary to carry this vote into effect."

This vote was passed while it was yet a question as to whether the town could legally appropriate money for such purposes. but the town was guaranteed against loss by liberal subscriptions by some of our patriotic citizens. These subscription papers are still in existence. and show that a large proportion of the citizens subscribed to this fund in amounts varying from $5 to $200 each, and the money was actually paid over to the committee. and afterwards refunded by the town.

In the following Spring. at the annual town meeting, the state having authorized it, it was voted: "That the Selectmen be authorized to borrow money if necessary to conform to the law for paying aid to the families of soldiers in the U. S. service." On the 25th of September, 1862, it was voted: "That we as a town vote to pay all those who have or shall enlist under the last two calls of the Government for troops, $100 each to be paid on their being mustered into service." On the 27th of Sept., 1862, it was voted, "That the sum of $100 be paid to each man who has enlisted, as nine months volunteers." This vote was passed because more men had volunteered than had been called for. Dec. 16th of the same year, it was voted: "To enter into an arrangement with other towns in this vicinity to establish an agency, for the purpose of communicating with the soldiers, and forwarding supplies for their comfort." Edwin A. Cooley was chosen as agent of the town in the matter, and $200 was raised to meet the expenses. This led to the forming of a "Soldier's Aid Society," and large quantities of articles, needful for the soldiers, were made and sent to the front, by means of which the men were greatly encouraged, and no doubt many lives saved.

At the annual meeting in 1863, under the ninth article: "which is to see if the town will pay bounty to any soldiers who enlisted from the town prior to July 1862," it was voted: "To defer action on the whole action for one year, except in the case of Charles M. Whitmore, a soldier who enlisted prior to that time, he having been wounded, disabled and discharged from service before he had served two years." That bounty was never paid to him.

By the middle of the year, 1864, it became more expensive to obtain men for the army, but all points of law had been settled, and recruiting very much simplified, and the town passed a final vote, which should cover the rest of the war, no matter how long it lasted, as follows: " Voted, that the Selectmen be authorized to borrow such sums of money as they deem proper, to fill all drafts that may be made upon the town hereafter."

The effect of these several votes by the town, and the efficient efforts of the Selectmen, were to encourage our young men to volunteer and fill the quota of the town, so that when, at the end of the war, an examination was made, it was found that Sunderland had filled its quota of 77 men, and had a surplus of eight, over and above all demands, making 85 men that had enlisted to the credit of the town.

The first call for soldiers was on the 16th of April 1861. for three months men. No man went from Sunderland on this call, and in fact only one man from Franklin Co. (he was from Northfield, named Frederick K. Field.) The second call was for three years men, and it began to look like more serious work. The first men that went from Sunderland enlisted in the 10th regiment, which was mustered in, June 21, 1861, and contained 9 Sunderland men. viz.: Abram C. Puffer. Chas. G. Blodgett, Chas. S. Hartwell, Samuel Graves, John W. Jones, John Heminway. Geo. A. Whitmore, David Lakeman, and Chas. M. Whitmore. This regiment went into camp at Springfield, and left the state July 25. 1861, and took part in the following battles: Fredericksburg, Chancellorsville. Gettysburg. Rappahannock Station, Wilderness, Spottsylvania, North Anna River, Cold Harbor, and the several engagements on the Peninsula. Then the 27th regiment went forward on Nov. 2nd of the same year. In this regiment went the following five men, viz.: Stillman D. Clark, Ransom D. Pratt, Thomas O. Amsden. William Farrell, and Hiram Pierce. This regiment took part in the battles of Roanoke, Newbern, Cold Harbor and nine others in North Carolina and before Richmond.

Then the 37th regiment left the state Sept. 7th, 1862, taking with it 9 more Sunderland men, viz.: Frederick L. Bagg, Ebenezer F. Wiley, Martin S. Hubbard, George D. Whitmore, James Clary, Edward A. Mahogany, Reuben E. Bartlett, Geo. L. Cooley, and Frederick B. Crocker. This regiment took part in the following engagements: Fredericksburg, Mayre's Heights, Salem Heights, Gettysburg, Rappahannock Station, Wilderness, Spottsylvania, Cold Harbor, Winchester, Petersburg, Fort Stedman, Opequan,

Hatcher's Run. and Saylor's Creek. This regiment was armed with the Spencer repeating rifle. captured three stands of rebel colors, and lost 248 men killed and died of wounds and disease.

Then came the call for 300,000 nine months men. In the 52nd regiment were 24 Sunderland men. Their names are as follows: J. M. Armstrong. Wm. F. Bowman, John R. Banks, Leander Brigham, Israel Childs, Jesse L. Delano. Alden Gilbert, Henry J. Grover, Parker D. Hubbard. Geo. W. Miller, Swan L. Lesure. A. Smith Munsell. Merrick Montague, Arthur Montague, Edgar J. Pomroy, Austin N. Russell. Chas. L. Russell, J. Wiley Russell. James W. Stebbins. Chas. A. Sanderson, Quartus Tower. James R. Warner, James B. Whitmore, and Henry Wilder. This regiment went into camp at Greenfield in Sept., 1862. was mustered into the U. S. service on the 11th of the following month, and after a season of busy drill and preparation, it joined the expedition under Gen. Banks, left Greenfield on the 19th of Nov., and proceeded to New York and then to New Orleans, serving in that department till the Mississippi River was opened for navigation its entire length, and was *the first regiment* that passed up that river on its homeward route. This regiment was kept in active service during the summer of 1863, leading the advance in the first attack on Port Hudson, and also being in the battle of Indian Ridge and the memorable assault on Port Hudson on the 14th of June. It also was subjected to some extremely hard marching, in one instance a march of 98 miles in four consecutive days. forty miles being performed during one day of twenty-four hours. The 52nd regiment lay in the trenches around Port Hudson at the time of the seige twenty-four days and nights, until its final surrender on the 8th of July. when the regiment started for home, arriving here on the 3d day of August, and was mustered out of the service Aug. 14, 1863.

There were other men from our town who also enlisted in several regiments at different times during the war; their names are as follows: Albert Rensellaer Dickinson White, Martin Van Buren Flagg, Charles Woods, Charles Daland Dean, Richard Newhall Blodgett, Elliott David Puffer, Erastus Ellsworth Andrews, Edwin Wright Ball, Thomas Archibald and James Hill.

This completes the list of Sunderland men who are supposed to have enlisted and served on the quota of the town; the number is 57. Edwin W. Ball re-enlisted, and counting him as another man on the quota the number is 58.

The remaining 27 men were secured by the selectmen from Boston and other places by the payment of bounty money, usually about $100, but in some cases a much larger sum was necessary, in one instance over $500. We have obtained the names of 15 of these men, viz.: Andrew Carter, Otto Peterson, James Harrington, John Howarth, Geo. H. Page, John Walsh, John Riley, David Labonne, Geo. N. Chamberlain, Geo. H. Chappel, Arthur Richie, Chas. Schlevoit. James P. Thorne and Robert Williams. The two last mentioned were colored men and served in the navy. These fifteen added to the quota swells the number from this town to 73. As yet no record has been obtained of 12 of the whole number of Sunderland men credited by the state.

There were, also, during the war, eleven young men, at least, former citizens of our town, who enlisted to the credit of other towns, and they deserve honorable mention in our Record. Their names are as follows: Brainard Montague, Thomas Lyman Munsell, Charles Munsell, Otis D. Munsell, Charles Fairchild, Henry D. Bartlett, George M. Williams, E. Baxter Fairchild, Myron D. Clark, Emory P. Andrews,

and Henry Church.   Again, there were a few men here who
were so situated that they could not leave those dependent
upon them, and yet desirous to do something to carry forward the war they paid liberal sums to secure others to go
and fight in their places.   These men deserve credit, for
they did what they could, and showed a willing spirit.
Four men *only* were drafted from our town, who were *patriotic* enough to go to the war, but on account of some
dependent ones, whom they could not leave, they provided
substitutes by the payment of liberal sums of money.
These men also deserve much credit, for they took upon
themselves, in some cases, a burden of debt, which it took
years to repay.   Two of our men were commissioned Lieu-
tenants, four were Sergeants, five were Corporals, and eight
others were appointed to important positions of responsibility,—and each and every one performed his duty with
fidelity, and was honorably discharged, and no one of them
has been convicted of any crime whatsoever since the war.
Ten of them still reside here, 26 "sleep the sleep that
knows no waking," and the rest are scattered from Vermont
to Texas, and from Connecticut to Oregon.   The history of
the labors, privations, marches, battles, and adventures by
land and sea, of each of them, if written out, would fill a
volume, and unless written will never be told, for only a few
more years will pass before they will all have passed away.

In the following pages will be found brief sketches of the
Sunderland men, incorporating in them a small part of the
facts that have been obtained, and which will be found in
full on record in the Town Clerk's office.

EDGAR JOSIAH POMROY, son of Erastus and Maria Pomroy,
was born in Sunderland Oct. 20th, 1839.   He lived at
home till he attained his majority, engaged with his father,
who was a farmer, and attended school.   At the time of his
enlistment he was a clerk in the store of Horace Lyman.

He enlisted Aug. 27th, 1862, in the 52d regiment, Co. G., and after about a month spent in camp at Greenfield was mustered into U. S. service Oct. 11, 1862, for nine months. He was appointed Sergeant. and was so faithful and efficient in the performance of duty that when the office of Orderly Sergeant became vacant soon after, he was appointed to fill that position, which he did with much credit. He was always on duty, never in hospital, never fell out on a march, and fairly earned a higher station in the regiment, being a favorite with all the men in his company, and at the close of the service two Bibles having been given to the Chaplain for the two best soldiers in the regiment, *he* received one of them. He was mustered out on the 14th of Aug., 1863. He was single when in service. but shortly after his return to civil life he removed to Holyoke, where he married and still resides.

ISRAEL CHILDS, son of Alvan and Sophia Childs, was born in Deerfield Jan. 27th, 1824, where he lived until he was about 21 years old. He then emigrated to the Wabash, (then considered the " far west") but when the California gold fever broke out in 1852, he took passage in a sailing vessel around Cape Horn, and after a voyage of *five months*, reached the land of gold. He spent four years in mining, and experienced the various vicissitudes incident to that rough life. Having had " tolerable " luck, he returned to Mass. in 1856 and purchased the farm where he now resides. In 1862 he enlisted in Co. G., 52d regiment, being mustered in on Oct. 11, and he went to Louisiana, where he proved to be an excellent soldier, his mining experience having been a good school to prepare him for camp life and the exigencies of an army campaign. He was often called upon to advise and assist those who were sick, and his devotion to a sick comrade nearly cost him his own life, for he became sick himself and was barely able to come home with the regiment.

He recovered however, and still lives (1880) to " fight his battles over." by the domestic fireside.

EDWARD AUGUSTUS MAHOGONY, son of John and Cordelia Mahogony, was born in Sunderland Oct. 17, 1841. He lived at home in the south part of the town until the time of enlistment Aug. 1. 1862, being then nearly 21 years of age ; was mustered into the 37th regiment, Co. F., Aug. 30, 1852. He was chosen a member of the color guard (a position of great responsibility and danger) where he served faithfully in the 16 battles and other skirmishes of that hard-worked regiment without being wounded, though often being the target for the enemy's rifle. He returned home after three years service with the regiment, and was mustered out June 21, 1865. He now resides in Westmoreland, N. H., engaged in farming.

JOEL MASON ARMSTRONG, son of Martin and Mary Mason Armstrong, was born in Wendell Nov. 21, 1833. He was a carpenter by trade and came to Sunderland before the war. He enlisted Sept. 5, 1862, in Co. G., 52d regiment, and was mustered into service Oct. 11, 1862. Being strong and in good health he endured the campaign well, especially the hard marching, never being obliged to " fall out." He was never obliged to go into hospital, though he was excused from duty a few days because of illness. Came home with the regiment and was mustered out Aug. 14. 1863. He still lives in Sunderland, and has held responsible offices for several years in both town and church.

GEORGE LEMUEL COOLEY, son of Charles and Mary Cooley, was born in Sunderland. Nov. 6, 1839. He always resided in Sunderland on the place where he was born. He enlisted in July, 1862, as a private for 3 years, and was mustered into the 37th regiment, Co. F., Aug. 30, 1862. He served continuously for the whole term in all the battles of that regiment and was never wounded. He was detailed a part

of the time as a Marker, in which capacity he was active
and efficient. Although never very strong physically, his
faithfulness in the discharge of all duty, and endurance of
fatigue in marching and other severe service, is remembered
and admitted by his officers and comrades. He was mustered out with the regiment June 21, 1865. He has since
resided on the paternal homestead, where he is still living.

QUARTUS TOWER, son of Orrin and Polly Tower, was born
in Chesterfield Aug. 14, 1822. Lived in Sunderland several
years previous to the war. He was mustered into the 52d
regiment Oct. 11, 1862, and served in the ranks for the full
time of enlistment, and was mustered out Aug. 14, 1863,
which was his 41st birthday. He lived here after the war
till 1870, when he removed to Granby. He died Dec. 7,
1875, of heart disease, which he thought was primarily
induced by his army life.

HENRY WILDER, son of Levi and Sarah Wilder, was born
in Wendell May 22d, 1842, but was living in Sunderland
when he enlisted in the 52d regiment in 1862. He went
with the regiment to Louisiana, and served faithfully for
the full term, and returned home with the rest, but in a
rather poor state of health. He was a carpenter by trade,
and after he returned from the army he went to Orange and
was employed in a chair shop. He there received a severe
injury on the hand, which became a very serious affair, and
from which he suffered extremely. His lungs also being
somewhat affected, he failed rapidly, and died April 12,
1869. He was buried in our cemetery.

WILLIAM FRANCIS BOWMAN was son of William and Tirzah
Bowman, born in Shutesbury May 1st, 1824; lived in Sunderland a large part of the time before the war, and enlisted
in the 52d regiment, Co. G., (nine months men) as a private
on the 28th of Aug., 1862, and was mustered into the U.
S. service Oct. 11th, following. He was detailed as cook

for the company, and was a general favorite among the men
of the regiment, by whom he was familiarly known as
" Major Bowman." He served the full time of his enlistment and was mustered out with the regiment Aug. 14th,
1863. He afterwards removed West, and died at Dixon,
Ill.. Jan. 1st. 1877.

MARTIN SCOTT HUBBARD, son of Chester and Amanda
Hubbard. was born at Northfield Farms Nov. 15. 1841. He
was living with David Hubbard when he enlisted in the
37th regiment. He was a large muscular man of superior
strength, and the tallest of the Sunderland men in that
regiment. An excellent soldier, enduring march and battle •
without exhaustion, but was the first of them to fall by the
shot of the enemy. He was killed at the battle of Spottsylvania May 12. 1864, by a minie ball through the neck.
cutting off the large arteries, so that he lived only a few
minutes. He was buried afterwards where he fell.

WILLIAM FARRELL was a boy taken from New York city
by F. H. Williams with whom he was living at the time of
his enlistment. Nothing is known of his birth or parentage.
He was mustered into the 27th regiment. Co. C., Sept 20,
1861, giving his age as 18 years, and served in the arduous
campaigns of that regiment in North Carolina and before
Richmond, taking part in at least fifteen battles. On the
16th of May. 1864, he was taken prisoner at Drury's Bluff.
Va. He was taken to Libby prison, from there to Andersonville. Ga., arriving there May 30. He was removed to
Charleston. S. C.. Sept. 13 ; removed to Florence, S. C..
Oct 1st, and suffered there till Nov. 16. when he and four
others enlisted in the Rebel army on condition of being let
out of prison. At Andersonville he became moon-blind, and
had to be led whenever he went out in the night. Nov. 21
he went into the rebel hospital, with three of his compan-
ions, and never has been heard from since. These facts

were obtained from Hart E. Morey of Leyden, a fellow-prisoner who survived and still lives. (1881).

JOHN W. JONES, son of Evan and Elizabeth Jones, was born in Wales, Great Britain, Apr. 30th, 1838. His mother died when he was four months old, and he came to this country when he was six years old with his father, who settled in York State, Lewis County, but after 10 years moved to the town of Hermon, St. Lawrence Co. He came to Sunderland and was living with D. Dwight Whitmore in 1861, and after the other men had gone away in the 10th regiment, he made up his mind to go on and join the same regiment, and was mustered into Co. K on the 5th of Sept. He was a soldier who endeared himself to his comrades, and was anxious to serve his adopted country in her extremity, and in his last letter to his father wrote that he " would fight the Copperheads as long as he could breathe rather than yield." He did fight manfully in those severe battles for nearly three full years, but on that terrible day —the 5th of May, 1864—on which the 10th regiment lost 115 men, killed and wounded, he was among those who fell, only two months before the regiment was mustered out of service, and he was buried on the ground that he died to redeem from secession.

ABRAHAM CINCINATTUS PUFFER, son of Harriet and David Puffer, was born in Montague Sept. 1, 1844. He spent most of his childhood and youth at home in No. Sunderland where his father lived. He enlisted Apr. 22d, 1861, in the 10th regiment, and was mustered into service the following June as a private for three years. He was 16 years old when he joined the army. Sailed from Boston and went to Washington, arriving there the 29th of July. On their march into and through the city to the place where their camp was to be, he was nearly overcome by the heat; he never was well after it, and was obliged to be taken to Columbia Hospital

in that city, where he died of fever Nov. 28th, 1861. The
men of his company sent his remains home, and they are
buried in the cemetery at No. Sunderland.

THOMAS OSBORN AMSDEN, son of Thomas O. and Susan
Amsden, was a native of Greenfield, born May 17. 1837.
His father soon after moved to Bernardston, and again back
to Greenfield in 1845, so that the time of his boyhood was
mostly spent in these two towns. He came to Sunderland
and was living with Quartus Sykes in 1862, when he
enlisted for three years. and was mustered into the 27th
regiment on the 10th of March, but after severe exposure
in service he was attacked by remittent fever and died at
Beaufort, N. C., on the 10th of September following, leaving
a wife and one child. His widow afterwards married Richard Loomis, and they reside in North Leverett.

HIRAM PIERCE, son of Jacob and Elizabeth Pierce, was
born in Shutesbury in 1820, but has been an inhabitant of
our town for many years, and enlisted in 1861, being mustered into Co. D, 27th regiment, Sept. 20th. He was in
two engagements, viz.: Newbern and Little Washington,
but was afterwards appointed cook for his company. Aug.
4, 1863, he was transferred to the Veteran Reserve Corps,
in which he remained until the expiration of his term of
service, and was mustered out Sept. 27, 1864. He owns
and still lives (1881) on the same place in Sunderland that
he occupied before the war.

JESSE LEMUEL DELANO, son of Ansel C. and Persis S.
Delano, was born in Sunderland Aug. 31, 1835, and lived
in the town most of the time till enlisting, in August,
1862. He was mustered into the 52d regiment, Co. G,
Oct. 11, 1862. Was in all the service of the regiment, was
never sick or wounded, and came home to be mustered out
at Greenfield Aug. 14, 1863. He still resides in Sunderland, (1881.)

AUSTIN NASH RUSSELL, son of Austin and Roxanna Nash Russell, was born in Sunderland Aug. 8, 1841, and lived at home till his enlistment, Aug. 28, 1862, in Co. G, 52d regiment, for nine months, being mustered into service of the U. S. at Greenfield Oct. 11, 1862. He went forward with the regiment to Louisiana, and served in the ranks till after a hard march on a hot day, when three-fourths of the men fell out by the way (he being one who did not) he was taken with a fever and obliged to go to the hospital at Baton Rouge. After a severe sickness of two weeks he was sent to the convalescent camp, and was detailed clerk of that camp, having charge of the books, and also assisting in removing the wounded from the boats as they arrived from the various battle fields to the hospitals to which they were assigned. He remained in this position, discharging its duties with ability, till after the surrender of Port Hudson, when he again joined his regiment, and with it returned to be mustered out at Greenfield Aug. 14, 1863. In 1866 he married Susan L. Sanderson, and afterwards removed to Shelburne Falls where he still lives, engaged in the marble business.

ERASTUS ELLSWORTH ANDREWS, son of Erastus and Almira Andrews, was born in Shelburne May 17, 1837. His father was a Baptist clergyman and removed to Sunderland while his son Erastus was quite young. He lived there until the time of his enlistment, Dec. 2, 1863, on which day he was also mustered into the 2nd battery of light artillery as a corporal for three years. He served the full time, and helped to secure the honors which have been so generally accorded to that battery, and was mustered out Aug. 11, 1866. He now resides in the town of Woodford, Vt., engaged in farming. He is a brother of ex-Governor Andrews of Conn.

JAMES RICHARD WARNER, son of Seth and Marmy Warner, was born in Sunderland Dec. 13, 1823, and resided in the town till his enlistment, which occurred Aug. 28, 1862. He went into camp at Greenfield and was mustered into the 52d regiment as a corporal in Co. G, Oct. 11, 1862. He went to Louisiana, and participated in the Gen. Banks' campaign, and though absent from duty sometimes on account of sickness, he was able to serve the full time and come home to be mustered out with the regiment. In 1866 he moved to Washington Territory, where he still lives, (1880,) in the township of White Salmon.

DAVID LAKEMAN, son of Adam and Rebecca Lakeman, was born in Ipswich Dec. 24, 1819. He was living at David Hubbard's in Sunderland when he enlisted. He was mustered into the 10th regiment, Co. G, as private for three years, May 1, 1861, but on account of disability was mustered out Jan. 26, 1862. After being mustered out he lived in So. Deerfield and Ipswich. He went to the Centennial Exposition in 1876, and his friends have heard nothing from him since.

CHARLES LOOMIS HARTWELL,, son of Obed and Lucretia Hartwell, was born in Conway May 31, 1843, where he spent his youthful days. At the time of the war he was living in Sunderland, and enlisted from our town, and was mustered into the 10th regiment, Co. I, Sept. 12, 1861, for three years. Served in that regiment until June 20, 1864, when he was transferred to the 37th regiment, from which regiment he was mustered out Sept. 12, 1864. He now lives at So. Amherst.

CHARLES MONTAGUE WHITMORE, son of Charles and Julia Whitmore, was born in Sunderland April 19, 1841. He enlisted in the 10th regiment April 22, 1861, in the company which was formed at Greenfield, and was mustered in with the rank of corporal. He was in two general battles

—one at Williamsburg, May 5, 1862, and the other at Fair Oaks, Va., May 31, 1862, where he was severely wounded—twice by minie-balls and the third time by buckshot, all within two minutes, and then as he afterwards lay upon the field came near being bayonetted like many other wounded men. He was taken to the hospital after the battle, where he lay until the 31st of October, 1862, when he was discharged and returned home. He has, however, never fully recovered from his wounds, and though partially disabled by them, never regrets that he did his part towards suppressing rebellion. He now resides in Meriden, Conn.

CHARLES AUGUSTUS FAIRCHILD, son of Curtis and Miranda Fairchild, was born in Sunderland, Sept. 8, 1845, and lived there during his boyhood. In 1862 (he then being 17 years old) he was very desirous of enlisting, but not being very strong, and also *under* the legal age of a volunteer, his friends did not wish him to enlist; but his brother, Rev. E. B. Fairchild being mustered into the 34th regiment as Chaplain Aug. 8, 1862, entitled by army regulations to have a servant, took Charles with him in that capacity. He went on with the regiment, which joined the army of the Potomac, just after the second battle of Bull Run. Owing to the confusion of the time they were obliged to bivouac without tents for a few weeks, and the exposure incident to this mode of life, so different from what he had been accustomed to, induced an attack of dysentery, of which he died, after an illness of about five days, on the 8th of Sept. 1862, that being his 17th birthday. His remains were brought home and buried in our cemetery.

RANSOM DICKINSON PRATT, son of Stillman and Eleanor Pratt, and grandson of Ransom Dickinson, formerly of this place. He spent a large part of his childhood and youth here with his grandfather, and at the time of the war was in Amherst College. He belonged to the college military company and the whole company offered their services to the state, immediately on the breaking out of the war, and he was mustered into the 27th regiment, Co. D on the 18th of Sept., 1861, for three years. He participated in the battles of Roanoke Island, Newbern, Kingston and Golds-boro. He served as Surgeon's clerk and assistant at Newbern, and was detailed to duty for considerable time in the Medical Purveyor's Office, and also in the Adjutant General's Office. In this capacity he was assigned to duty on board a vessel loaded with medical stores, and made a trip to Florida. He was then detailed to duty on a hospital steamer for treating and transferring wounded soldiers on the coast. He rounded the stormy Cape Hatteras eleven times in his trips back and forth during the war. At Newbern he assisted in establish-ing educational work among freedmen, in Sunday and evening schools, being on duty away from regiment at close of serv-ice. He was mustered out alone, exposed to yellow fever at Newbern he came near falling a victim, but reached home, by short stages, and delays of sickness, at N. Y., Fortress Monroe and Fall River, and nearly died after reaching home, having chills and fever for several months. He now resides in Marlboro, Mass.

ELLIOT DAVID PUFFER, son of David and Harriet Puffer, was born in Sunderland Aug. 21, 1847, and lived there at home till the time of enlistment in the 34th regiment, being mustered in Dec. 30, 1863, for three years. He went to Harpers Ferry, the regiment being there at the time of his enlistment, and spent the winter in that vicinity, in various camp duties, making one or two short trips in the country south with foraging parties, etc., but in the spring took part in active service. On the 15th of May the sanguinary con-flict of New Market occurred, and in that battle he was taken prisoner with a few others of various regiments, and after many changing places of confinement he was finally sent to the prison pen at Andersonville—the place most dreaded of all, by captured men—and after *five months* of hardships, exposure to sun and rain, and, worst of all, *starvation*, he died on the 12th of Nov., 1864.

ANSON SMITH MUNSELL, was a son of Thomas E. and Roxanna Munsell. He was born in Sunderland Oct. 3d, 1836. He was attending school at Bernardston when the war broke out, but left there to enlist in the 52d regiment. He was appointed corporal in this regiment and served with honor through its campaign in Louisiana, returning home in Aug., 1863, and also to his studies. The next year he again enlisted in the 61st regiment for three years, and was commissioned Lieut. by Gov. Andrew. He was present at the storming of Petersburg and marched into the city the next morning, his regiment taking the lead in the column. When the war was over he took a three years course in medicine, since which he has been quite successful in Chicago as a physician where he now resides.

JAMES BIRNEY WHITMORE, son of Chas. and Julia Whitmore, was born in Sunderland June 19, 1843. He enlisted in the 52d regiment, and was appointed Corporal; served the full time, without losing a day, and came home with the regiment. He again enlisted in the 30th Unattached Co., heavy artillery, and was appointed Corporal, but while at Fort Smith, Va., he was promoted to the place of Sergeant after a sharp competitive examination for excellence in drill and other soldier-like qualities, and remained in service till the close of the war. He now resides in Holyoke.

GEORGE WASHINGTON MILLER, son of Washington and Fanny Miller, was born in Salisbury, Vt., July 8, 1843. His father afterwards moved to this place, and Geo. lived here till the time of his enlistment into the 52d regiment, Co. G, for nine months. He went to Louisiana and followed the fortunes of the regiment without accident till the siege

of Port Hudson where he was wounded in the hand by a
rebel bullet, while on duty in the trenches, whereby he lost
one finger. He came home with the regiment, and was mustered out Aug. 14, 1863. He now resides in Chicago, Ill.

EBENEZER FARWELL WILEY, son of Ebenezer and Adaline
Wiley,was born in Sunderland Jan. 12, 1840. He was mustered into the 37th regiment July 27, 1862, being then 22 years
of age. He was in the various severe battles of that regiment, and was promoted to the position of Corporal and
then of Sergeant, on account of faithfulness and bravery.
On the 21st of August, 1864, near Charlestown, Va., he
was wounded in the head by a rebel bullet which fractured
the skull. He was taken to the hospital, and after a time
recovered and reported for duty once more. He was then
transferred to the Veteran Reserve Corps, in which he remained the rest of the three years. He still lives in Sunderland, but will always carry on his head visible evidence
of his army life.

FREDERICK LUTHER BAGG was a member of the 37th regiment, and took an active part in a score of hard-fought
battles,and was thought a very efficient soldier, and although
much exposed he never was wounded. He was especially
commended for bravery at Petersburg, where in the midst
of a general engagement he, single-handed, surprised and
captured a small fort containing about 25 men. They, sup-
posing him to be well-supported, threw down their arms;
but before he could receive assistance a re-enforcement came to
their aid, and he was obliged to retreat, which it is said he
did in good order, with "drums beating and colors flying,"
of course. He now resides in So. Deerfield.

JAMES WHITNEY STEBBINS, son of Eben and Rebecca Stebbins, was born in Deerfield May 17, 1838, and was living
in Sunderland previous to the war; enlisted on the 27th of
Aug., 1862, and was mustered in as first sergeant of Co. G,

52d regiment, nine months men, Oct. 11, 1862. He went to Louisiana and participated in the first attack on Port Hudson, and also in the occupation of Plaquemine, but was taken sick, and being discharged for disability June 11, 1863, he returned home in a feeble condition, but finally recovered, and after a few years removed to Springfield where he has since resided, being employed as an express messenger on the Conn. River railroad.

CHARLES DALAND DEAN, son of Charles and Abby Dean, was born in New Salem June 9, 1843. His father soon after moved to Sunderland and his early years were spent in this town. He was, however, living in Oakham when the war came on, and he enlisted from that town in Co. II, 25th regiment, Sept. 24, 1861, for three years. He was discharged Jan. 18, 1864, and he re-enlisted from Sunderland Jan. 19, 1864, in the same regiment. He was detailed as cook, and for hospital duty, and filled these difficult positions with ability and success; was mustered out July 13, 1865, having been in the army nearly four years. He now lives in Boston.

CHARLES ALBERT SANDERSON, son of Horace and Emily Sanderson, was born in Sunderland Aug. 4, 1842. His parents removed to Ludlow, but on the death of his father Charles came back to this town, being then eight years of age. He lived ten years afterward with Albert Montague, Esq., and enlisted in Co. G, 52d regiment, as a private, Aug. 12, 1862, and was mustered in Oct. 11, for nine months. He served through the whole campaign and returned with the regiment to be mustered out Aug. 1, 1863. He was single when in the army but has since married; lived for a time in No. Dana, but has returned to his native town, where he now resides.

HENRY JOSIAH GROVER, son of Josiah and Mary H. Grover, was born in Hadley May 27, 1833. His early years up to the time of the war were spent in this town, his father having removed here in 1839. He enlisted in Co. G, 52d regiment, and was mustered in, Oct. 11, 1862, and served the full term of enlistment with the regiment, being in the first attack on Port Hudson, at Plaquemine and at Oak Bend. He came home with the regiment, was mustered out Aug. 14, 1863, and has since lived, most of the time in this town, but at the present time is in Amherst where he keeps a popular boarding house.

JOHN HEMINWAY was born in 1843, of English parents, and when quite young was consigned to the almshouse at Monson, from which place he was taken by Dea. Elihu Heminway of North Leverett, to whom he was bound by the name of John Burns, in 1855. He lived with Mr. Heminway till 1860. He then came to Sunderland and was living here at the time of enlistment, and was mustered into the 10th regiment, June 21st, 1861, as a private for three years, in Co. G. He re-enlisted Dec. 21st, 1863, and followed the fortunes of that regiment till June 20, 1865, when he was transferred to the 37th regiment and June 21, 1865, again transferred to the 20th regiment, where he served till mustered out, July 16, 1865, making more than four years of continuous service. He is still living somewhere in Vermont, though he has lived in Montague some time since the war.

MARTIN VAN BUREN FLAGG, son of Jeremiah and Clarissa Flagg, was born in Conway July 12, 1844. When he was quite young his parents moved to this town, where his boyhood was spent at school, at general farm work, and at his father's steam saw mill. He was mustered into the 18th regiment, Co. A, as a private for three years, Sept. 21, 1861. He took part in the second battle of Bull Run, and other service near Washington, was obliged to be mustered out for disability, Nov. 27, 1862, having served a little over one year. His ancestors landed at Plymouth in 1636, and some of them served in the Revolution with distinction. He was single when in service but has since married, and is now living at North Amherst.

CHARLES WOOD, at the time of the war was living in this town with Henry J. Graves. Nothing is known of his birth or parentage, he having been taken from Westboro by William W. Russell, who was his guardian. He enlisted and was mustered into the 20th regiment, Co. D, Aug. 23, 1861, for three years, served in the ranks for the full term and was mustered out Aug. 30, 1864. He was at the battles of Fredericksburg, second battle of Bull Run, the seige of Knoxville, Spottsylvania, and some other engagements in Virginia, including the battles at Petersburg, where he won the commendation of his officers for good service.

ALBERT RENSSELAER DICKINSON WHITE, son of David and Belinda White, was born in Hadley Dec. 14, 1837, where his youthful days were spent. He was living with Sidney S. Warner in this town when he enlisted. He was mustered into the 31st regiment, Co. F, Nov. 7, 1861, as a private for three years, sailed from Boston with Gen. Butler's command, arrived at Ship Island, and went from thence to New Orleans. But exposure to wet and cold brought on rheumatism, and he was discharged from service July 10, 1862. He returned home, but afterwards removed West, and finally South, and is now (1880) living at Running Brushy, Texas.

RICHARD NEWHALL BLODGETT, son of Leonard and Mary Blodgett, was born in Conway Aug. 30, 1837. His life before the war was spent mostly in Conway, Deerfield and Sunderland, where he worked at farming. He enlisted Nov. 12, 1862; was mustered into the 32d regiment, Co. C, for three years, as a private, Nov. 27, 1861. He participated in the battles before Richmond in 1862 and at

Antietam, but was mustered out for disability Dec. 22, 1862.
Returning home he moved to Warwick, where he now
resides. He was never wounded, but has always suffered in
health from effects of army life.

JAMES CLARY was a native of Ireland, and came to this
country in 1849. He went immediately into the employ of
Horace Lyman of this town, and has resided here ever since
with the exception of his army life. He was mustered into
the 37th regiment Sept. 2, 1862, and served to the end of
the war. He was detailed as officer's servant most of the
time; was mustered out June 21, 1865, and still lives in
Sunderland.

STILMAN DEXTER CLARK, son of Eliphalet and Flavilla
Clark, was born in Sunderland Nov. 3, 1821. He lived in
Sunderland most of the time previous to his enlistment.
He was mustered into the 27th regiment, Co. D, as a private,
for three years; on the first of Sept., 1865, went to North
Carolina, and remained in the vicinity of Newbern most of
the time he was in service. He did not participate in any
of the great battles, but was in some of the skirmishes, and
on those hard marches which *used up* so many of the men.
He was mustered out for disability Sept. 27, 1864, since
which time he has lived in this vicinity and now resides in
South Deerfield.

PARKER DOLE HUBBARD, son of Ashley and Betsey Hubbard, was born in Sunderland May 15th, 1825, on the paternal
homestead in the south part of the town, which was the
home of his grandfather, Maj. Caleb Hubbard, a patriot of
the Revolution. He enlisted in Co. G, 52d regiment, Aug.
20. 1862, and was mustered into U. S. service Oct. 11 following. He served in the ranks some of the time, but was
detailed to take charge of some important foraging expedi-
tions, which duty he performed with much credit. He
returned home with the regiment and was mustered out

Aug. 14, 1863. He has since married and lives on the old homestead, engaged in farming. He has also acquired quite a reputation as a breeder of fine driving horses.

THOMAS LYMAN MUNSELL, son of Thomas E. and Roxanna R. Munsell, was born in Sunderland Oct. 13, 1831. At the time of the war he was a merchant in Ashfield, and enlisted for that town being mustered into the 1st regiment cavalry, Co. II, for two years, on the 14th Aug., 1862, and followed the fortunes of war, without any wounds or severe sickness, till he was mustered out at the expiration of service, Nov. 11, 1864. He now resides in Holyoke.

OTIS DORRANCE MUNSELL, son of Thomas E. and Roxanna Munsell, was born in Sunderland Sept. 8, 1838. He lived in our town most of his life previous to the war, and was well known to our citizens. He enlisted, however, for the town of Montague, having moved there a short time before. Was mustered into the 22d regiment, Co. I, July 15, 1863, as a private for three years. Otis was at the battles of Rappahannock Station and Mine Run in 1863, and several engagements in the Wilderness in the spring of 1864, where he received wounds of which he died on the 7th of May, 1864.

CHARLES LEONARD RUSSELL, son of Emmons and Myra Russell, was born in Sunderland April 8, 1858, and lived in town till the war. He enlisted in Co. G, 52d regiment, Aug. 27, and was mustered into service, Oct. 11, 1862, at Camp Miller, Greenfield. Served through the campaign in Louisiana, and returned to be mustered out at Greenfield Aug. 14, 1863. He was never sick or wounded, and was an efficient soldier and a good comrade. He returned home and engaged in farming, and having married resides on the paternal homestead.

FREDERICK BEAL CROCKER was a son of Zaccheus and Climena Crocker, and was born in Sunderland July 27, 1836.

He spent his childhood at his home in the south part of the town. He enlisted and was mustered into the 37th regiment Aug. 30, 1862, as a private in Co. F, for three years. He was detailed as a pioneer, in which position he was very efficient and able, having worked at the carpenter's trade previous to his enlistment. But though his duties called his attention mainly to other things, he always kept his gun handy, was ready to assist in repelling an assault or to aid in an attack, and took part in many of the sharp battles of 1863 and the early part of 1864. On the 21st of June, 1864, near Petersburg, Va., while engaged in putting up the tents for the night after a skirmish with the enemy, he was struck by a stray bullet, which caused his death. He was one of the best soldiers in that noble regiment, and his loss left a gap in the ranks not easily filled. His remains were brought home and are buried in the cemetery at North Amherst.

HENRY STEVENS CHURCH, son of Henry and Judith Church, was born in Sunderland Sept. 12, 1835. At the age of fifteen, his father died and he went to Biddeford, Me., to learn the machinist's trade, but his eye-sight failing him he returned and lived a while with his mother at Belchertown. They afterwards removed to a house on the west bank of the Connecticut a short distance above Sunderland bridge. He enlisted in the 31st regiment and was appointed a Sergeant. He was suddenly taken sick on the 24th of May, 1862, and died of typhoid fever on the 31st of the same month. He was married in Nov., 1859, to Miss Vesta Barber, of Portland, Me. He enlisted for Belchertown.

THOMAS ARCHIBALD, was a young man—the youngest who enlisted from this town—being only fourteen years old. He came from the state almshouse at Monson to live with Quartus Sykes. Nothing is known of his early life, or of his parentage, thorough examination at the almshouse and at Boston having revealed nothing in regard to either. He joined the 34th regiment on Jan. 2d, 1864, the regiment being then in the defenses about Washington. In December following the regiment went further South, and young Archibald took part in two quite severe battles, viz.: Hatcher's Run and in front of Petersburg, and was commended by his fellow soldiers for his bravery. In the latter engagement, however, he received a wound in the thigh, and was taken to the U. S. General Hospital at Fortress Munroe, where he died on the 26th of April, 1865, and was buried in the Hospital cemetery with Christian ceremony and military honors.

Edwin Wright Ball, son of Silas and Jerusha Ball, was born in Sunderland July 6, 1838, and lived a large part of the time at home. in the south part of the town, till the war broke out. He was at work at his trade as carpenter in Amherst at that time, and enlisted on the 20th of February, 1862, in Co. L, 1st regiment, heavy artillery with the rank of private. He was present at the second battle of Bull Run. and some other slight engagements. This regiment was kept most of the time in the vicinity of the Capital for garrison duty. On the 22d of February, 1864, he was discharged to re-enlist as artificer, which he did the next day in the same regiment. and to his honor, be it said, that he preferred to re-enlist for his own town, even though he was offered a much larger bounty from another. After some severe labor and exposure in July and August of that year, he was taken with fever, and after a short sickness he died at City Point, Va.. Sept. 10, 1864. His body was removed to North Amherst for burial.

Charles Graves Blodgett, son of Leonard and Mary Blodgett, was born in Deerfield Feb. 4th, 1844. His father moved his family to this town and Charles was living at home at the time of the commencement of the war, working

with his father at the mason's trade, being then 17 years of
age. He was enthusiastic in regard to the great conflict,
and desirous to take part in it. Having obtained the con-
sent of his parents, he entered the 10th regiment, and was
mustered in, June 21st, 1861, as a private, and afterwards
promoted to the position of Corporal. He left Boston with
the regiment on the 25th of July, and by steamer reached
Washington the 30th. They soon after crossed the Potomac, and he took part in the hard work of the regiment,
never being sick a day; never off duty, which, consider-
ing his age, was worthy of mention. He took part in the
battles on the Peninsular, Fredericksburg, Chancellorsville,
Gettysburg, Rappahannock Station, and the numerous severe
battles of the Wilderness up to the 18th of May, 1864,
when, after nearly a month of hard marching and fighting,
he was taken prisoner, nearly three years after he enlisted.
In all this danger and exposure, he never lost his conviction
that the Union would be maintained, and though ever among
the foremost of his rank, he never was wounded. He was
taken to Andersonville prison only three days before his
time would have expired, where he spent six weeks of suf-
fering and misery, being inhumanly treated and half starved.
He became weak and thin, and finally quite unwell; but
there came a prospect of an exchange of prisoners, and he,
with other, was taken to Charleston, S. C., for that purpose.
Hope again revived, and he began to look forward to the
time when he should once more see his native town. But
the exchange was deferred, postponed, and then refused,
and the disappointment was so great that our hero lost his
ambition and courage, and soon died at the Charleston City
Hospital. In the words of a comrade he was "a good
soldier, a faithful friend, a loyal patriot, and a martyr to his
country."

BRAINARD MONTAGUE, son of Warren and Beda Montague, was born in Sunderland May 20th, 1841. He spent his early years in this town, assisting his father on the farm, attended school, and afterwards learned the carpenter's trade. In 1861 he went to Amherst, N. H., to attend school, and while there he was strongly impressed that it was his duty to enlist in the army. He went to Manchester and enlisted Dec. 14th, and was mustered into the 8th New Hampshire regiment, Co. E, Dec. 31st, 1861, as a private. He had entertained the idea of some day becoming a doctor, and was immediately detailed to duty as an assistant in hospital work. In that capacity he went to Ship Island, but the heat and crowded condition of the barracks brought on typhoid fever, from which he died May 4, 1862, after an illness of only one week. His First Lieutenant speaks of him as " earnest and zealous as a soldier, watchful, efficient and tender as an assistant, and one from whom they had expected much."

ARTHUR MONTAGUE, youngest son of Warren and Beda Montague, was born in Sunderland Mar. 15, 1843, and lived at home most of the time till he enlisted. He was mustered into the 52d regiment, Oct. 11th, 1862, and went to camp anxious to do his part in the suppression of the Rebellion. On the voyage from New York to New Orleans, however, the men were all very sea-sick, and in his case it seemed to lead into erysipelas, and he was quite sick before his arrival at Baton Rouge, on the 17th of Dec., and he was obliged to enter and stay in the hospital, afflicted alternately with erysipelas and rheumatism, till on Feb. 27th, there being no probability of his recovery under such circumstances, he was discharged, and on the 2d day of March he started for home accompanied by his brother Merrick. They arrived home March 25th, but diphtheria

L. & C.

set in and he died on the 2d day of April, 1863, only a week after reaching home.

HENRY DEXTER BARTLETT, son of Dexter and Clarinda Bartlett, was born in Sunderland June 17th, 1844. He lived here in town during his childhood and youth, but at the time of the war he was living in Springfield, where he was employed at the machinist's trade, to which he was ardently devoted, and in which he hoped to excel. But he heard his country's call and enlisted in the 46th regiment, Co. A, for nine months, and went with the regiment to Newbern, N. C., in September, 1862, arriving there Nov. 15, and went immediately to outpost duty at Newport Barracks, an important station between Newbern and Beaufort. He was always ready for duty, and energetic in action, and made many friends in the regiment. But he was taken sick with putrid typhoid fever, and after only a short sickness, died on the 9th of February, 1863. He was brought home by some of his comrades, and laid to rest in our cemetery by the river.

GEORGE DWIGHT WHITMORE, son of Chas. and Julia Whitmore, was born in Sunderland Aug. 31, 1839. He resided at home most of the time, being well known throughout the town, and was a young man of much promise. He enlisted in the 37th regiment, in July, 1862, and went into camp at Pittsfield, being mustered in on the 30th of August. He was naturally strong and robust and endured the hard service of march and field better than most men, and took part in all the battles in which the regiment was engaged during 1862, '63 and '64, and also in the work of suppressing riots in New York City. But on April 2d, 1865, while at the battle of Petersburg, engaged in carrying forward a quantity of ammunition, he was struck upon the head by a piece of a shell. It was hoped that he would recover, but after a few days he grew worse and was sent to the hospital at

Washington, arriving there on the 12th of April, and died on the 14th. His body was brought home and funeral services were held in the church, and he was buried in the quiet cemetery at No. Sunderland. A fellow soldier said of him, " He was a brave man among the bravest, and a general favorite among his comrades."

SWAN L. LESURE, son of Ansel and Polly Lesure, was born in Warwick Jan. 14, 1827. He was living in Sunderland in 1862 when the call came for 300,000 nine months men, and took an active part in gathering together and organizing Co. G of the 52d regiment, which was composed almost entirely of Amherst and Sunderland men. He was mustered in, Oct. 11, 1862, as Lieutenant of that company, but for certain reasons was mustered out before the regiment left the state. He afterwards enlisted in another regiment, and died while on picket duty near Petersburg, Va., June 21, 1864.

MERRICK MONTAGUE, son of Warren and Beda Montague, was born in Sunderland Nov. 19, 1834. His father resided in the south part of the town, on the road to Hadley, and Merrick spent his childhood and youth there. On arriving at years of maturity he took up the carpenter's trade, at which he was engaged when the 52d regiment of nine months men were called for. His brother Arthur having a great desire to enlist, this was probably a strong inducement for him to enlist in the same company, that they might be a help to each other, if need be. They enlisted, were mustered in, and went into camp together at Greenfield, went to New Orleans and Baton Rouge with the regiment, arriving at New Orleans on the 14th of Dec., 1862. On the voyage he had been obliged to take care of his brother Arthur who was quite sick, and continued to do so after their arrival at Baton Rouge on the 17th. The confinement and anxiety began to tell upon his own health, and when

Arthur was discharged and sent home Merrick was permitted to accompany him. On arriving home he immediately went to Boston and obtained his discharge for disability, on the 1st of April, 1863. But army life and its burdens, both physical and mental, had undermined his naturally robust constitution, and though for some few years he was able to attend to business, he never fully recovered, and being attacked by consumption he died on the 28th of Nov., 1866. He was much beloved by his soldier comrades, and respected by his townsmen, who honored him with the office of Selectman, in the year 1865. He left a wife and one child, who still reside in Sunderland (1881).

ALDEN GILBERT, son of Jervis and Mary Gilbert, was born in Leverett Sept. 3, 1844, where he lived till, at the age of seventeen years, he came to Sunderland and lived with Dea. Elihu Smith to the time of his enlistment in the army, on the 27th of Aug., 1862, and was mustered into the 52d regiment, Co. G, as a private, Oct. 11, 1862. He went to Louisiana, and shared the hard service with the rest of the men, being at the siege of Port Hudson, at Oak Bend, Plaquemine, and New Iberia. He was obliged to go into the hospital for a short time at Baton Rouge, but recovered to come home and be mustered out Aug. 14, 1863. He was single when in the army, was married in 1870, and has since lived in Conway, but now resides in No. Hadley engaged in farming.

JOHN WILEY RUSSELL, son of Justin and Sarah Wiley Russell, was born in Sunderland July 9, 1830, and lived here most of the time until his enlistment, Aug. 21, 1862. He went into camp at Greenfield, and was mustered into Co. G, 52d regiment, Oct. 11. 1862. He participated in all the marches and hard work of that regiment, was never wounded nor seriously sick, took part in the battle of Oak Road and the assault on Port Hudson, came home with the regiment and was mustered out Aug. 14, 1863. Since the war he has been engaged in farming, in this town part of the time, but is now living at Amherst, where he is employed in the express business.

REUBEN EMERSON BARTLETT, son of Lemuel and Sophia Bartlett, was born in Shutesbury May 25, 1843. He lived there until he was fifteen years old, then in Leverett and Amherst two years, and afterwards in this town till he enlisted July 18, 1862; went into camp at Pittsfield, and was mustered into the 37th regiment, Co. F, Aug. 30, 1862, for three years. He was obliged to be in the hospital some on account of sickness, and was accidentally wounded by a blow from an axe at Brandy Station, but was nevertheless in several of the notable engagements with the enemy, and did efficient service, especially at the battle of Winchester, where he attracted attention for individual action and bravery. He has since suffered seriously from injuries received in the army, but has received a pension from the Government. He came home with the regiment and was mustered out June 21, 1865. He afterwards prepared himself for the ministry, and was Pastor of the Elm St. Baptist Church in Wilmington, Delaware, for one year, but his health failing, he was obliged to resign that useful position, and returned to this town, where he still resides.

LEANDER BRIGHAM, son of Joel and Elizabeth Brigham, was born in Deerfield March 23, 1823. He passed his early years in Deerfield, but at the time of the war was living in Sunderland. He had serious thoughts of enlisting early in the conflict, but delayed doing so until the call came for the 300,000 nine months men. He then went into the 52d regiment, Co. G, being mustered in, Oct. 11, 1862. He went to Louisiana, and shared the fortunes of the final campaign in that state, endured some of the hard marches, fatigue work and picket duty, but on account of sickness was obliged to go into the hospital for a season, after which he assisted in hospital work. He came home with his regiment, and was mustered out Aug. 14, 1863. He afterwards removed to Montague, where he now resides.

GEORGE MOSELY WILLIAMS, son of Oliver and Miriam Williams, was born in Sunderland Sept. 13, 1823. He spent his childhood and youth here, and a large part of his life also before the war, and was well known in our community. He had considerable literary attainments. and articles of his writing may now be found in the old files of the agricultural papers of Massachusetts. He enlisted in some New York regiment and came home after the war, without being wounded, though once obliged to be in the hospital for a short time. He died Sept. 19, 1872.

GEORGE ARMS WHITMORE, son of D. Dwight and Jane Whitmore, was born in Spring Prairie, Wisconsin, Apr. 15, 1840. His childhood and youth were spent at his home in North Sunderland, and he had just attained his majority when the guns of Fort Sumter roused the country to war, and he enlisted on the 18th of May, 1861. and was mustered into the 10th regiment on the 21st of June. He served his full term of 3 years. was in many hard fought battles, exposed to hardship and dangers innumerable, but was never wounded, nor was he ever kept from duty any length of time by sickness. Came home with the regiment and was mustered out on the 6th of July, 1864. He afterwards was employed on the New London Northern railroad, and was accidentally killed near Stafford Springs, Conn., July 2d, 1867,—almost exactly three years after his discharge from the army.

JAMES HILL, was living at David Hubbard's in the north part of the town, and enlisted in the 32d regiment. Co. A, as a private for three years, Sept. 3, 1863. He participated in the battles of the Wilderness, and did good service until the 12th of May, 1864, when at the battle of Laurel Hill he was fatally wounded and died the same day.

JOHN RANDOLPH BANKS was born in Ashfield Jan. 8, 1840. His parents were Orlando and Caroline Whitney, and he was named Francis Orlando Whitney. His father died soon after, and his mother gave him to John S. Banks of Bernardston, who adopted him as his own son, and had his name changed to John Randolph Banks. He spent most of his early years in Bernardston, but coming to Sunderland in 1859, he married Julia L. Dunklee, and resided here when the war broke out. When the call came for the 300,000 nine months men, he enlisted and was mustered into the 52d regiment, Co. G, as a private, Oct. 11, 1862. He was a good soldier, fearing no danger, and was always ready for duty. Mustered out August 14, 1863, after his full term of service in the swamps of Louisiana, he returned to Sunderland and engaged in farming. But he had become diseased, and subject to inflammatory troubles—probably increased by exposure and hardships in the army—which finally developed into a cancerous humor, from which he died on the 24th of June, 1869, and was buried in the cemetery at Sunderland. He left three children, two of whom still survive. His widow married James Farr of Greenfield, where they are now residing, (1881.)

SAMUEL GRAVES, son of Hubbard and Mary Graves, was born in Sunderland May 1st, 1839. He spent his early years in this town, and learned the trade of painting, of his father. When about 20 years old he went to Amherst to work with an older brother, but at the time of enlistment he was living in Belchertown. He was mustered into the 10th regiment, June 21, 1861. He served three full years, was in several engagements, and twice obliged to go to the hospital, was never wounded, and was mustered out with the regiment in July, 1864. He lived afterwards in Amherst most of the time till his death, which occurred Jan. 18, 1878. His remains were brought to Sunderland for interment.

EMORY PEARL ANDREWS, son of Rev. Erastus and Almira Bartlett Andrews (formerly of No. Sunderland), was born in Middlefield, March 28, 1830. His father preached for the Baptist Church at No. Sunderland for many years. Emory commenced to teach school in Montague in the winter of 1850—'51. He afterwards taught in the Academy at Shelburne Falls, and was Principal of the High School at the same place in 1856—'57. In 1858 he was installed as Principal of Hollis Institute at So. Braintree, Norfolk Co., where he remained till he entered the army. He enlisted as a private at Rowe, Franklin Co., Sept. 15, 1861, in the 31st Massachusetts regiment, but was chosen Second Lieutenant, and was mustered into Co. C, Nov. 20, 1861, for three years. He was promoted to a First Lieutenancy, Feb. 20, 1862, and was appointed Military Sheriff of the Department of the Gulf, attached to the staff of Maj. Gen. B. F. Butler, during his command in New Orleans. His duties in this position were exceedingly difficult. Among other matters of public importance he had charge of the execution of Wm. B. Mumford for high treason, in New Orleans, June 16, 1862. It will be remembered that Mumford was the only person hanged for high treason during the whole rebellion. He also executed four other men in the Parish prison of New Orleans by command of Gen. Butler. (These executions were deemed necessary by the Government to establish its authority and restore order). He was with Gen. Banks at the siege of Port Hudson and through the Red river campaign. He was three times wounded, though never seriously, and had a horse shot under him at Sabine Cross-Roads, La., Apr. 8, 1864. He served his full time and was mustered out Nov. 20, 1864. Returning home he removed to Rochester, N. Y., and was for several years principal of Genesee School in that city. For the ten years between 1870 and 1880 he was engaged in teaching music, associated with Prof. L. O. Emerson of Boston. He is now—June, 1881—President of the Conservatory of Music at Xenia, Ohio, and Sup't of music in the city public schools. He was "off duty" in the army only three days during the whole three years; and for more than twenty years as teacher has never missed a lesson, and never, as pupil or teacher, had a "tardy mark." He was a brother of Charles P. Andrews (also from this town) who was Governor of Connecticut in 1880.

MYRON DEXTER CLARK, son of Stillman D. and Lucy A. Clark, was born in Sunderland Apr. 9, 1848. Lived in Sunderland and North Amherst till the war. Enlisted Aug. 1st, 1866, for one hundred days, in the 60th regiment, Co. G, as a private. Served on the quota of Amherst. Spent most of his time in garrison duty at Indianapolis, Ind., guarding rebel prisoners. Mustered out, Nov. 30, 1864. He married Mary E. Thompson March 2, 1871, and settled in Alstead, N. H., where he now resides (1881) engaged in farming.

EDWARD BAXTER FAIRCHILD, son of Curtis and Miranda Fairchild, was born in Sunderland Sept. 15, 1835. He enlisted from Sterling in June, 1862, in Co. C, 34th regiment, Massachusetts volunteers, but before he was mustered into the U. S. service was elected as Chaplain of his regiment, and in that capacity mustered into the service, Aug. 8, 1862. His regiment was occupied in garrison duty about Washington for a year, when getting tired of this kind of service, he resigned his commission July 3, 1863, to accept a position of greater activity and usefulness in the " U. S. Sanitary Commission." As special relief agent he went through the Gettysburg campaign, helping to care for the

20,000 men wounded in that battle. He spent most of the winter of 1863—4 collecting vital statistics for the Sanitary Commission, in the vicinity of Washington, New York, and at the U. S. military prison at Point Lookout, Md. In the spring of 1864 he was ordered to Chattanooga, Tenn., and in May of that year started with Sherman's army on the Georgia campaign as relief agent for the 14th army corps. He went as far as Atlanta, but was prevented from going through to Savannah by sickness contracted from hardships and exposure in the Atlanta campaign, and came home to devote his time to lecturing in New York, Pennsylvania, Maryland and Delaware, to raise money for the Sanitary Commission. He remained in the employ of the Sanitary Commission to the close of the war. After the war he returned to the active duties of his profession. He was settled over the Unitarian church in Whately for two years and a half; removed to Stoneham, in 1868, where he had charge of the Unitarian church in that town and Reading for about ten years, when failing health compelled him to give up the work of the ministry for a time. Since 1878 he has been engaged in the book business, and is now connected with Lee & Shepard of Boston, but now resides in Stoneham, the town for which he enlisted. He was actively engaged in organizing the " Grand Army of the Republic," and was commander of the Stoneham Post for two terms.

We have thus given sketches of the service and army life of all those who went from Sunderland and served on the quota of the town, and also of many others who were residents or natives of the town, but who served on the quotas of other towns. It is not a complete record, but we trust it is correct as far as it goes. and we hope that as future generations peruse its pages it may serve to keep alive the memory of those who served the town and country in time of need. In addition to the above sketches, there is recorded in the town clerk's office the name of each soldier, the date and place of his birth, time of enlistment, time he was mustered into service, time of discharge or date of death, number of regiment and company, rank, names of parents, amount of bounty, and other facts that may be useful in the future to the soldiers, their descendants or to the town. The above-mentioned record will be kept by the town clerk, and whenever any additional facts are discovered they may be added in the proper time and place, and it is hoped that all friends of the old veterans will aid in making the record complete in all particulars.

INDEX.

Names of those who enlisted for Sunderland, who were residents of that town at the time of their enlistment :

INDEX.

Names of men who served to the credit of the town of Sunderland, that were obtained abroad, having never lived in Sunderland:

Andrew Carter,	36th.
George N. Chamberlain,	V. R. Corps.
George H. Chappel,	V. R. Corps.
James Harrington,	19th.
John Howarth,	24th.
David Labonne,	29th.

Names of men who had been or were residents of Sunderland that enlisted on the quota of other towns: